W9-BEB-371

Grammar Gremlins

An Instant Guide to Perfect Grammar
for Everybody in Business

Jean Rupp

BookPartners, Inc.
Wilsonville, Oregon

BookPartners, Inc.
P.O. Box 922
Wilsonville, Oregon 97070

Dedication

To my husband, Herb, whose support and encouragement made it possible for me to create the Grammar Gremlin.

And also to Fred — our "best friend."

The gleeful Grammar Gremlin gloats when he's "gotcha."

Table Of Contents

Grammar Gremlins

grem lin (grem´ lin) n. **1.** An imaginary gnome-like creature to whom mechanical problems, especially in aircraft, are attributed. **2.** A maker of mischief. [Perhaps blend of Irish *gruaimin,* bad-tempered little fellow (from middle English *gruaim,* gloom, surliness) and GOBLIN.]
   — *The American Heritage Dictionary of the English Language THIRD EDITION*

Grammar Gremlin (Gram´ r Grem´ lin) n. **1.** An imaginary roach-like creature to whom grammatical problems, especially in business writing, are attributed. **2.** A maker of mischief that infests business writing and contaminates it.
   — Jean Rupp

The New Roachettes – a chorus line of Grammar Gremlins – kick up their heels over your mistakes.

Introduction

Good writing is a powerful tool. It can make your message stand out from the mass of material that competes for attention every day. The problem with much business writing today, however, is that it is infested with Grammar Gremlins—those roaches that encroach upon your daily letters and memos to contaminate your message and alienate your reader. Business writing must be letter-perfect. You will commit "suicide-by-letter" if your communications have errors in grammar and usage. Therefore, you must exterminate Grammar Gremlins from every document you produce.

How good is your grasp of the English language? Do Grammar Gremlins plague the pile of papers on your desk? To help you find out, test your knowledge by answering the following questions:

Grammar Gremlin Check-up

1. Do you write *good,* or do you write *well?*
2. Is it *Send the letter that you wrote* or *Send the letter which you wrote?*
3. Should you say *It is I* or *It is me?*
4. Do you feel *bad* or *badly* about choosing an incorrect answer?
5. Is it *Who did you talk to yesterday* or *Whom did you talk to yesterday?*

(See page 4 for answers.)

If you don't know the answers to all the questions, don't feel bad (not *badly).* Many people have problems with the basics. And it's not surprising. The English language is not an easy language to master. In addition to that, our language is changing. Many of the grammar rules of 50 years ago simply don't apply today. So what are you supposed to do?

One thing you can do is become familiar with the most common Grammar Gremlins. Once you know them it will be easier to exterminate them from your communications. Learn them well and make sure the pesky creatures don't ravage your written words.

That is why I wrote this book—to help you as a busy professional avoid these easy-to-make errors with little effort on your part. It is organized into a simple, easy-to-understand reference guide.

Part I defines all the parts of speech and all the parts of the sentence, citing examples that will help you in your daily writing responsibilities. Additionally, it lists 35 common word usage problems.

Part II provides a list of the 25 most common errors in grammar made by business people. I have created the list from the thousands of memos, letters, reports and proposals I have read as a communications consultant and writing instructor for business and government.

If you learn just these top 25 errors in grammar and exterminate them from your writing, you will dramatically improve the correctness of your documents.

The added benefit is that you will not only make yourself look good to customers and colleagues, but you will also make your organization look good. What you put on paper makes a powerful impression. Make sure yours is a superior one.

Happy Grammar Gremlin hunting! Apply these basic principles to your business writing and watch the Grammar Gremlins scamper from the page.

ANSWERS TO THE GRAMMAR GREMLIN CHECK-UP: 1. *well* (Grammar Gremlin # 13, p. 88)   2. *that* (Grammar Gremlin # 4, p. 70)   3. It is *I* (Grammar Gremlin # 3, p. 68)   4. *bad* (Grammar Gremlin #12 , p. 86)   5. *Whom* did you talk to yesterday? (Grammar Gremlin # 6, p. 74)

Make those pesky Grammar Gremlins scamper
from your page.

Part I

The Parts of Speech

Nouns
Pronouns
Verbs
Adjectives
Adverbs
Prepositions
Conjunctions
Interjections

The Sentence and Its Parts

Subjects
Predicates
Phrases
Clauses
Simple Sentences
Compound Sentences
Complex Sentences
Types of Sentences
Word Usage Problems

The Parts of Speech

Grammar classifies the words that compose sentences as "parts of speech." They are the building blocks of our language. Understanding how they function is at the core of knowing how to make sentences work for you.

Grammar Gremlins like to confuse the parts of speech in your mind so that you make mistakes when you write. I've defined the parts of speech to prevent you from getting mixed up. Whenever you are in doubt, just refer to these simple definitions.

What Are the Eight Parts of Speech?

1. **Nouns** name things.
2. **Pronouns** take the place of nouns.
3. **Verbs** express action or state of being.
4. **Adjectives** modify nouns or pronouns.
5. **Adverbs** modify verbs, adjectives, or other adverbs.

6. **Prepositions** show the relationship between their objects and other words in the sentence.
7. **Conjunctions** connect words, phrases, and clauses.
8. **Interjections** express strong feelings.

Some words can function as more than one part of speech. Their purpose in the sentence determines the part of speech.

Nouns

A noun is a word used to name a person, place, thing, or idea.

Kinds of Nouns

1. A **common** noun names a person, place, or thing without being specific: *man, city, company.* Common nouns are not capitalized.

Kinds of Common Nouns

- A **collective** noun names a group or collection, but it is considered singular: *committee, people, crowd.*
- A **concrete** noun names something material or tangible: *bone, bowl, water.*
- An **abstract** noun names a quality or idea: *hunger, loyalty, devotion.*

2. A **proper** noun names a specific person, place, or thing: *David Doberman, Portland, Bowser Beefy Dog Food Company.* They are capitalized.

Uses of Nouns

Nouns can function in sentences as:

- Subjects *(The **meeting** ended.)*
- Objects of verbs *(David wrote the **memo.**)*
- Objects of prepositions *(He sat in the **chair.**)*
- Predicate nominatives *(Ben is my **assistant.**)*
- Appositives *(Fred, my **dog,** chased the ball.)*
- Nominatives of address *(**Jean,** please speak up.)*

Pronouns

A pronoun is a word that acts in place of, or on behalf of, a noun. There are six different kinds.

Kinds of Pronouns

- **Personal pronouns** refer to a person or persons. Personal pronouns have 30 case forms.

  Definition of case: The form of a noun or pronoun that indicates its relationship to other words in the sentence.

Singular

	Nominative (Subject)	Possessive	Objective (Object)
1st person	*I*	*my, mine*	*me*
2nd person	*you*	*your, yours*	*you*
3rd person	*he, she, it*	*his, her, hers its*	*him, her it*

Plural

	Nominative (Subject)	Possessive	Objective (Object)
1st person	*we*	*our, ours*	*us*
2nd person	*you*	*your, yours*	*you*
3rd person	*they*	*their, theirs*	*them*

- **Relative pronouns** relate or connect the clauses they introduce to the independent clause. *Who, whose, whom, which,* and *that* are frequently used.

    The Bowser Beefy dog treats *that* we introduced last month have sold remarkably well.

Whoever, whenever, whichever, and *whatever* are less frequently used.

- **Demonstrative** pronouns point out or identify nouns or other pronouns. Examples are *this, that, these,* and *those.*

    These are our newly improved Doggy Delights.

    This should certainly capture the market.

- **Interrogative** pronouns ask questions. They are *who, whom, whose, which, what* and occasionally *whoever, whichever,* and *whatever.*

    > *Who* is our sales representative for California?
    >
    > *Whom* did they expect to convince?

Confused about when to use *who* and *whom?* This Grammar Gremlin frustrates many writers. Read page 74 to exterminate it from your writing.

- **Indefinite** pronouns give a general or indefinite impression. Among the most frequently used are *all, another, any, anyone, anything, everybody, everyone, everything, few, many, nobody, one, several, some,* and *each.*

    > *Nobody* attended the meeting last month.
    >
    > Iris Setter sent a memo to *everyone* in the department.

- **Reflexive** pronouns are compounds of personal pronouns with *-self* or *-selves.*

    > David *himself* tested the new Bowser Beef Bites.

They assigned *themselves* to the project before anyone else could volunteer.

Verbs

A verb is a word that expresses action *(speak, write, listen)* or state of being *(is, am, are, was, were, be, being,* and *been.)*

Kinds of Verbs

Let's look at verbs in two different categories: (1) regular and irregular and (2) transitive, intransitive, and linking

Category 1: Regular and Irregular Verbs

Regular verbs form the past tense and past participle by adding *-ed, -d,* or *-t* to the present tense.

listen	*listened*	*listened*
hear	*heard*	*heard*
deal	*dealt*	*dealt*

The past participle in a sentence with a regular verb would look like this:

> David Doberman *has scheduled* a sales meeting.

Irregular verbs form the past tense and past participle by changing a vowel of the present tense or by other changes in spelling.

speak	*spoke*	*spoken*
write	*wrote*	*written*
go	*went*	*gone*

The past participle in a sentence with an irregular verb looks like this:

> David Doberman *has written* the agenda.

Category 2: Transitive, Intransitive, and Linking

A **transitive** verb requires an object to complete its meaning. In other words, a noun or pronoun follows it and completes the action specified by the verb.

He *read* <u>the</u> <u>report</u> carefully.

David *prepared* <u>the</u> <u>proposal</u>.

An **intransitive** verb expresses a complete action without an object. In other words, a noun or pronoun does not need to follow it to make complete sense of the sentence.

He *read* until late.

David *won* easily.

A **linking** verb shows the relationship between the subject and the noun that follows it, sometimes called the predicate noun.

David Doberman *became* the president.

Sometimes a linking verb shows the relationship between the subject and an adjective following it, sometimes called the predicate adjective.

Iris Setter *seems* preoccupied.

The most common linking verb is *to be (is, am, are, was, were, being,* and *been)*. Other frequently used linking verbs are *appear, become, feel, grow, look, remain, seem, smell, sound,* and *taste.*

More About Verbs

What About Auxiliary Verbs?

Auxiliary verbs are helpers. They serve as assistants to the main verbs in sentences. Examples are *be, do, may, have, shall, will.*

> Rex Shepherd *is* <u>promoting</u> our new line of Doggone Doggy Delights.
>
> My dog, Fred, *has* <u>drooled</u> over every morsel of those Delights.

What Are the Principal Parts of Verbs?

The English language has three principal parts of verbs: present tense (present infinitive), past tense, and past participle.

Present	Past	Past Participle
decide	*decided*	*decided*
sit	*sat*	*sat*
eat	*ate*	*eaten*
put	*put*	*put*
think	*thought*	*thought*

What About the Other Tenses?

Future tense denotes action that will take place in the future.

> Spuds *will attend* the meeting tomorrow.

Present perfect tense denotes action completed at the present.

> Spuds *has attended* the meeting.

Past perfect tense denotes an action completed before some indicated time in the past.

> Spuds *had attended* the meeting.

Future perfect tense denotes action that will be completed before a certain time in the future.

> Spuds *will have attended* the meeting.

What Other Properties of Verbs Are Important?

Voice is important. Voice refers to whether the subject of a sentence acts or is being acted upon. Verbs can be in either the active or the passive voice.

Active voice presents the subject as the doer of the action.

>Randy Rottweiler presented the proposal.

Passive voice presents the subject as the receiver of the action.

>The proposal was presented by Randy Rottweiler.

Mood is important. Mood refers to exactly that—a state of mind. It presents how the writer wants a statement made: as a fact, as a request, as a command, as a condition, or as a probability. Verbs can be in three moods: the indicative, the imperative, or the subjunctive.

The **indicative** mood states a fact or asks a question. Most sentences are in this mood.

>Fred loves Canine Crunchy Chewies.
>Why does Fred love Canine Crunchy Chewies?

The **imperative** mood expresses a request, command, or order.

Sit down. Stay. Fetch.

You is the understood subject.

A note to writers: When writing instructions, use imperative sentences.

The **subjunctive** mood expresses a doubt, an improbable or impossible condition, or a wish.
He acts as if he *were* president.
If I *were* you, I would ask for a raise.
I wish I *were* going.

A note to writers: When using the state of being verb (see verb definitions), use *were* with all three persons in the subjunctive mood.

Adjectives

An adjective is a word that modifies or describes a noun or a pronoun.

> These *tasty* treats will sell fast. *(Tasty* modifies the noun *treats.)*
>
> Fred grabbed the *tasty* one. *(Tasty* modifies the pronoun *one.)*
>
> These treats are *tasty. (Tasty* is a predicate adjective modifying *treats.)*

What About Articles?

The adjectives *a, an,* and *the* are sometimes called articles.

Adverbs

An adverb is a word that modifies or describes a verb, an adjective, or another adverb. It generally tells *how, when, where, why, how often,* and *how much.*

Fred barked *loudly. (Loudly* modifies the verb *barked* and answers *how.)*

Fred let out an *exceedingly* loud bark. *(Exceedingly* modifies the adjective *loud.)*

Prepositions

A preposition is a linking word used before a noun or pronoun to show its relationship to some other word in the sentence. Some common ones are:

about	*beside*	*in*	*since*
after	*by*	*of*	*under*
at	*for*	*on*	*up*
before	*from*	*over*	*with*

The preposition with its object is called a prepositional phrase.

Rex Shepherd presented the proposal *during the meeting* .

Is it correct to end a sentence with a preposition? Check Grammar Gremlin #21 on page 104.

Conjunctions

A conjunction is a word used to connect words, phrases, and clauses. There are two kinds: coordinating and subordinating.

Coordinating conjunctions connect words, phrases, and clauses of equal rank. Common ones are *and, but, or, for, nor, yet,* and *so.*

Coordinating conjunctions used in pairs are called **correlating** conjunctions. Those most frequently used are *both...and, either...or, neither...nor, so...as, whether...or,* and *not only...but also.*

Subordinating conjunctions connect dependent clauses to main clauses. Common ones are *if, since, because, that, which, although,* and *until.*

Interjections

An interjection is a word that expresses strong feeling. It is independent of the sentence. Most writers will not use it much. Examples are *Wow! Ouch! Ah! Yipes!*

These parts of speech are the foundation on which we structure our language to create clear and effective sentences. They are the building blocks of communication. Learn them well!

Other Terms Useful to Know

Verbal

A verbal is a word derived from a verb, but it functions as a noun, adjective, or adverb. The three verbals are gerunds, participles, and infinitives.

Gerunds are words derived from verbs ending in *-ing,* but they function as nouns.
Selling takes skill and fortitude.

Participles are verb forms that serve as adjectives.
Freezing rain snarled traffic.

Infinitives are the form of the verb preceded by *to.* They can function as nouns, adjectives, or adverbs.
To speak in public is difficult for Randy.
He begged for some water *to drink.*
Randy was happy *to learn* the speech was canceled.

The Sentence and Its Parts

The sentence is a group of words that contains both a subject and a predicate and expresses a complete thought. Several elements form sentences.

What Are the Parts of a Sentence?

The two essential parts of a sentence are the subject and the predicate.

<u>Subject</u> / <u>Predicate</u>

Connie Chow / conducted research on dog nutrition.

Carol Collie / documented the research.

The woman in the front office / laughed out loud.

Subject

The subject is the person *(who)* or thing *(what)* the sentence is about.

> *Jack Russell* made an exciting announcement.
>
> *Bowser Beefy Dog Food Company* excelled in sales last month.

The **simple subject** is the particular word or words—the noun or pronoun alone.

> All the *people* in the room stood and cheered.

The **complete subject** is the simple subject with all its modifiers.

> *All the people in the room* stood and cheered.

The **compound subject** is two or more words usually connected by *and* or *or*.

> *Rex and Iris* received sales awards

Predicate

The **predicate** says something about the subject; it tells what is being done. It makes a statement of action or state of being.

> Jack Russell *made an exciting announcement.*
>
> Bowser Beefy Dog Food Company *excelled in sales last month.*

The **simple predicate** is the particular word (or words) that expresses the action or state of being. It is the verb.

> The announcement *thrilled* the sales manager.

The **complete predicate** is the verb (simple predicate) with all its modifiers.

> The announcement *thrilled the sales manager.*

The **compound predicate** consists of two or more verbs usually connected by *and* or *or.*

> The announcement *thrilled and delighted* the sales manager.

A **complement** is a word or group of words that completes the action in the predicate.
> The announcement thrilled and delighted *the sales manager.*

Back to Sentence Definitions

Another way to define a sentence is to say it is made up of two basic word groups: phrases and clauses.

Phrases

A **phrase** is a group of words that does not have both a subject and a predicate. However, it could have one or the other. It does not express a complete thought.

There are two kinds of phrases: prepositional phrases and verbal phrases.

Prepositional phrases start with a preposition and modify other words. They can function as adjectives or adverbs.

> Ben Beagle stepped *into the room.*
> The advertisement *for Beefy Big Bites* caught their attention. (adjective phrase)
> They decided to invest *in our stock.* (adverb phrase)

Verbal phrases are introduced by a participle, a gerund, or an infinitive.

Adjusting his tie, Lou Labrador walked to the head of the table. (The participial phrase functions as an adjective.)

Convincing the committee was difficult. (The gerund phrase functions like a noun—the subject.)

The committee members listened carefully *to hear Ben's message.* (The infinitive phrase functions as an adverb in this sentence.)

Clauses

A **clause** is a group of words having a subject and a predicate. Clauses are of two kinds: independent and dependent.

An **independent clause** (also known as a main clause) expresses a complete thought and can stand alone as a sentence.

Linda Newfoundland presided over the meeting.

A **dependent clause** (also known as a subordinate clause) does not express a complete thought and cannot stand alone even though it has both a subject and a predicate.

Because Linda Newfoundland presided over the meeting.

A "signal" word (subordinating conjunction) attaches it to a main clause.

<u>*Because*</u> *Linda Newfoundland presided over the meeting,* it ran smoothly.

Common Subordinating Conjunctions "Signal" Words

after	*if*	*unless*	*whatever*
although	*since*	*until*	*which*
because	*that*	*when*	*who*

Dependent clauses can function as nouns, adjectives, and adverbs.

What she said was thought-provoking. (noun)

The new slogan *that Linda presented to us* captured our attention. (adjective)

We will use the slogan *if the committee approves it.* (adverb)

Don't commit suicide-by-letter.

How Are Sentences Structured?

Structurally, sentences can be simple, compound, complex, or compound-complex.

Simple Sentence

A **simple sentence** is a group of words that has both a subject and a verb and expresses a complete thought. It is one independent clause.

Fred tasted our new Frosty Paws.

It can have more than one subject and more than one verb, but all the subjects must perform all the actions in the predicate.

Fred and *Fido tasted* our new Frosty Paws and *loved* every bite.

Simple sentences many times contain one or more phrases within the independent clause.

Licking his chops, Fred tasted our new Frosty Paws. (introductory participial clause)

Fred, *my dog,* tasted the new Frosty Paws. (appositive phrase)

Compound Sentence

A **compound sentence** contains two independent clauses. The independent clauses can be joined one of three ways:

1. Use a comma with a coordinating conjunction *(and, but, or, for, nor, yet, so)*.

    Bowser Beefy Dog Food Company plans to open a branch office in Memphis, *and* Stan Bernard will be the manager.

2. Use a semicolon (;).

    The new office will open April 1; we hope everyone will be able to attend the grand opening.

3. Use a conjunctive adverb—a transitional word like *additionally, therefore, however, moreover, consequently, on the other hand,* and *similarly.*

Place a semicolon (;) before it and a comma (,) after it.

We plan to strengthen our position in the dog food industry; *therefore,* we need to plan a more aggressive marketing strategy.

Complex Sentence

A **complex sentence** contains an independent clause with one or more dependent clauses.

> *Carol Collie makes an excellent research assistant because she studied nutrition in college.*

In the example above, the dependent clause *because she studied nutrition in college* comes at the end of the sentence. Therefore, do not use a comma.

If, however, the dependent clause comes at the beginning of the sentence, place a comma after it.

> *Because she studied nutrition in college,* Carol Collie makes an excellent research assistant.

Sometimes the dependent clause comes in the middle of the sentence.

• If the clause includes essential or defining information, do not use commas.

> The report *that Carol wrote* provides valuable information on canine nutrition.

• If the clause includes non-essential or non-defining information, place commas around it.

> Carol's report on canine nutrition, *which she completed this morning,* provides valuable information.

Compound-Complex Sentence

A **compound-complex** sentence contains two or more independent clauses and one or more dependent clauses.

> *The potential buyers from Seattle, who arrived by limousine, attended the presentation; they liked what they heard about the new Bowser Beefy Doggy Delights.*

Types of Sentences

A Declarative Sentence

This sentence makes a statement; it declares something. A period follows it.

> Bowser Beefy Dog Food Company captured the market with creative new products.

> David Doberman spoke confidently to the board members.

An Interrogative Sentence

This sentence asks a question. A question mark follows it.

> Who designed the new logo?

> When will the sales meeting end?

An Imperative Sentence

This sentence makes a command or a request. It usually has an understood "you" subject and ends with a period. If it is an especially strong command, it may end with an exclamation point.

Bring me last month's figures.
Send a congratulatory memo to Stan Bernard.

An Exclamatory Sentence

This sentence expresses strong feeling. It usually ends with an exclamation point.

Congratulations!
That's a terrific idea!

Get rid of this naughty Roachette, appearing daily
in your written words.

Grammar Gremlins Infest Words Too
35 Common Usage Problems

A lot – alot

A lot (meaning a considerable quantity) is always two words, not one—*alot*.

Thanks *a lot* for your help.

For effective style, it's better to choose a different word or words in formal writing.

Thank you *so much* for your help.

Affect – effect

Affect is normally used as a verb meaning "to influence, change, assume." *Effect* can be either a verb meaning "to bring about" or a noun meaning "result, impression."

The decision will not *affect* (change) our marketing policy.

We will assess the full *effect* (result) of our decision to change the Bowser Beefy television commercial.

We must *effect* (bring about) immediate improvement in the quality of Bowser's products.

All right – alright

Spell *all right* as two words. *Alright* is non-standard English. Do not use it.

Already – all ready

Already means "even now" or "previously." *All ready* means "all prepared."

The committee *already* made the decision.

The committee is *all ready* to make a decision.

Among – between

Use *among* when referring to three or more.
Use *between* when referring to two.

> It was difficult to choose a winner *among* all the contestants.
> We must choose *between* the top two contestants.

Amount – number

Use *amount* for things in bulk or mass. Use *number* for individual items.

> We have a large *amount* of dog food in the warehouse.
> We still have a *number* of samples in the warehouse.

And etc.

Never use *and* before *etc*. The abbreviation of *et cetera* means "and other things."
You would be creating a redundancy.

Anxious – eager

Both *anxious* and *eager* can mean "desirous," but *anxious* also implies fear or anxiety. Careful writers do not use them interchangeably.

> I'm *anxious* about the interview.
> I'm *eager* to begin my new job.

Assure – ensure – insure

Assure means to "give someone confidence." *Ensure* means to "make sure." *Insure* means to "protect against loss."

> I want to *assure* you that we will win the contract.
> I want to *ensure* that we will win the contract.
> I decided to *insure* my business for an additional amount.

Bring – take

Bring indicates motion toward the speaker. *Take* indicates motion away from the speaker.

> *Take* this proposal to the third floor.
> *Bring* me the proposal by noon.

Capital – capitol

Capital has three meanings:
1. A town or city that is the official seat of government

   Howard works in Washington, D.C., our nation's *capital.*

2. An upper-case letter

   Be sure to use a *capital* letter when you write a proper noun, like "Howard."

3. Money

   Howard is trying to raise some *capital* to start his own business.

Capitol is a building in which a legislature meets.

   The senate assembled in the *capitol.*

Complement – compliment

To *complement* means "to complete." To *compliment* means "to praise."

The new slides will *complement* your presentation.

Our president, David Doberman, gave you a nice *compliment* on your presentation.

Comprise -compose

Comprise means "to include, contain, consist of." *Compose* means to "make up."

Human Resources *comprises* three separate departments.

Three departments *compose* Human Resources.

Data-datum

Datum is the singular form. *Data* is the plural form; however, *data* may take a singular or a plural verb. *Datum* is falling out of general use.

When *data* is used in the sense of "information," it takes a singular verb.

The new *data* on canine nutrition *is* revolutionary.

When *data* is used to mean "separate pieces of information," it takes a plural verb.

> The *data* compiled by our four researchers *are* now being analyzed.

Disinterested – uninterested

Disinterested mean "impartial." *Uninterested* means "not interested" or "bored."

> Howard Huge was *disinterested* in our proposal to open a branch office in Richmond, Virginia. (He's impartial.)

> Howard was *uninterested* in attending the conference. (He's not interested in attending.)

Due to – because of

Due to introduces adjective phrases that modify nouns. It is most often used after a form of the verb *be. (is am, are, was, were, being, been)*

> Bowser Beefy's position in the industry is *due to* its commitment to quality. (*Due to* modifies the noun *position.*)

Because of introduces adverb phrases that modify verbs, adjectives, and other adverbs.

> David Doberman won top honors *because of* his excellent management style. *(Because of* modifies the verb *won.)*

Enthused

The verb *enthused* is not well accepted. Careful writers use *enthusiastic*.

> All of us are *enthusiastic* about the new Bowser Beefy ad campaign.

Farther – further

Farther indicates a measurable distance. *Further* means "to a greater extent."

> David's car is parked *farther* from the convention center than mine.
>
> We need to investigate our options *further*.

Fewer – less

Fewer refers to items you can count. Use it with plural nouns. *Less* refers to degree or amount. Use it with singular nouns.

> *Fewer* employees called in sick last month; therefore, we had *less* absenteeism.

First – firstly

In enumeration, use the forms *first, second, third*, etc., not *firstly, secondly, thirdly*.

Hopefully

Hopefully, means "full of hope." It is not correct to use *hopefully* to mean "I hope."

> INCORRECT: *Hopefully,* the meeting will begin on time.
>
> CORRECT: *I hope* the meeting will begin on time.
>
> CORRECT: The applicant looked at the personnel director *hopefully*.

Imply – infer

Imply means "to suggest"; *infer* means "to assume."

David Doberman *implied* that I won the contest.

David *inferred* from Connie's comment that he won the contest.

In – into – in to

In means "positioned within." *Into* means "entry or change of form." *In* can be used as a part of a verb phrase. *To* following it serves as a part of an infinitive.

My report on canine nutrition is *in* the basket.

Mary Spitz stepped *into* the office.

Mary came *in to* see me this morning.

Its – it's

Its is the possessive pronoun. *It's* is a contraction of *it is*.

Bowser Beefy, Inc., must launch *its* ad campaign soon.

It's too expensive.

Lay – lie

Lay (*lay, laid, laid, laying*) means "to put" or "to place." *Lie* (*lie, lay, lain, lying*) means "to recline, rest, or stay."

Lay the report on the desk.
She *laid* the report on the desk.
Mary needs to *lie* down and rest.
Yesterday, Mary *lay* down to rest.

May – can – might – could

May and *might* imply permission; *can* and *could* imply power or ability.

You *may* turn your application in tomorrow.
If you *can* complete the application now, leave it with my secretary.

Might of – could of – would of – should of

Of is incorrect after *might, could, would,* and *should.* Use *have* instead.

Fred *might have* been a famous dog.

More than – over

More than implies numbers

Bowser Beefy Dog Food Company, Inc., has *more than* 200 employees nationwide. NOT: Bowser Beefy Dog Food Company, Inc., has *over* 200 employees nationwide.

Over implies position.

The new advertising campaign pushed us *over* the top in sales.

Per - a

Do not use *per* to mean "in accordance with."

INCORRECT: *Per your request*, we are enclosing two copies of the documentation. BETTER: *As you requested*, we are enclosing two copies of the documentation.

Per, from Latin, is often used to mean "by the"—22 miles *per* gallon. Whenever possible, substitute *a* for *per*—22 miles *a* gallon.

Precede – proceed

Precede means "to go before." *Proceed* means "to go ahead."

Hard work *precedes* promotions.

Now we can *proceed* with our marketing plan.

Principal – principle

Use *principal* to mean "chief" or "most important." Use *principle* to mean "a rule" or "a truth."

David Doberman's *principal* objective is to provide excellent products with superior customer service.

David is a man of *principle*.

Shall – will

The helping verb *shall* has fallen out of common use except in the most formal writing.

Will is used more often. Follow these guidelines.

1. To express future tense:
   - Generally use *will* with all three persons (*I, we, you, he, she, it, they*).

     I *will* be happy to assist you.

     They *will* be happy to assist you.
   - In the most formal writing, use *shall* with first person (*I, we*) and *will* with second and third person (*you, he, she, it, they*).

     I *shall* be happy to assist you.

     He *will* answer all your questions.
2. To indicate determination, promise, desire, choice, or threat:
   - Generally use *will* with all three persons.
   - In the most formal writing, use *will* for first person and *shall* for the second and third persons.

     I *will* report you to our supervisor.

     You *shall* report it to our supervisor.

Supposed to

Spell *supposed* with a *-d*.

They were *supposed to* arrive by 3:00 p.m.

NOT: They were *suppose to* arrive by 3:00 p.m.

Their – there – they're

These are not interchangeable. *Their* is the possessive form of *they*. *There* is an adverb meaning "in that place." *They're* is a conjunction of *they are*.

Lou Labrador was *their* manager.

Place the research notes over *there*.

They're excited about attending the conference.

Use – utilize

Use means "to put into service" or "to apply for a purpose."

Betty Beagle can *use* her new screwdriver to tighten the screws on the door hinge.

Utilize means "to make use of" or "to find a purpose for."

Betty Beagle can *utilize* her knife to tighten the screws on the door hinge since she doesn't have a screwdriver.

Don't let pesky Grammar Gremlins take the bite
out of your message.

Part II

Top 25 Grammar Gremlins

Points of the Compass
Pronoun Reference
Pronouns *I* and *Me*
Pronouns *That* and *Which*
Pronouns *That* and *Who*
Pronouns *Who* and *Whom*
The Pronoun *Myself*
Indefinite Pronouns
Subject/Verb Agreement
Compound Subjects Subject/Verb Agreement
The Articles *A* and *An*
Bad and *Badly*
The Adjective *Good* and the Adverb *Well*
Sentence Fragments
Run-on Sentences
Dangling Participles
Misplaced Modifiers
Parallel Structure in Sentences
Parallel Structure in Lists
Not Only...But Also and *Either...Or*
Prepositions
Double Negatives
Numbers in Dates
Comparative and Superlative Degrees
Nonstandard Words

Grammar Gremlin #1

Misuse of Points of the Compass

When are they proper nouns?
When are they common nouns?
Let's stop the confusion with this one. I see this misused by business writers frequently.

Grammar Gremlin: Our new branch office is *South* of Memphis.

Exterminated: Our new branch office is *south* of Memphis.

Grammar Gremlin: Our new branch office is in the *south*.

Exterminated: Our new branch office is in the *South*.

Capitalize *north, south, east, west,* and derivative words when they designate specific regions or are an integral part of a proper noun.

the *South*	the *North* Pole
West Coast	out *West*
the Middle *East*	*East* Coast
Eastern Seaboard	the Deep *South*
down *South*	

Do not capitalize them when they designate direction or general location.

> Travel *south* on Chesapeake Parkway. (direction)
> Stan Bernard will move to the *South*. (region)

Grammar Gremlin #2

Misuse of Pronoun Reference

A pronoun must agree in number, person, and gender with its antecedent (the word for which the pronoun stands).

Grammar Gremlin: A manager must listen to *their* employees.

Exterminated: A manager must listen to *his or her* employees.
Managers must listen to *their* employees.

Grammar Gremlin: Stan Bernard selected Gray Hound to help him write the ad because *he* is creative.

Exterminated: Stan Bernard selected Gray
Hound to help him write
the ad because *Gray* is creative.

Whenever you use a pronoun, make sure the
reader knows to whom the pronoun refers. Look
out for vague and unclear references in groups of
sentences as well as within a single sentence. You
don't want to confuse your reader with these
Grammar Gremlins.

Grammar Gremlin #3

Misuse of the Pronouns *I* and *Me*

A pronoun must agree in case with its antecedent (the word for which the pronoun stands). Many business writers struggle with these troublesome Grammar Gremlins.

Grammar Gremlin: Jill and *me* scheduled the meetings.

Exterminated: Jill and *I* scheduled the meetings.

Use *I* when it is the subject or one of the subjects in the sentence. In other words, use the pronoun in the nominative case.

Grammar Gremlin: Connie Chow explained the new procedure to Lou and *I*.

Exterminated: Connie Chow explained the new procedure to Lou and *me*.

(Use the objective case. *Me* is the object of the preposition *to*.)

When a pronoun follows any form of the verb *to be (is, am, are, was, were, being, been)*, it should be in the nominative case.

Grammar Gremlin: The person who revealed the new slogan was *him*.

Exterminated: The person who revealed the new slogan was *he*.

When a personal pronoun occurs in a construction introduced by *than* or *as*, it should be in the nominative case.

Grammar Gremlin: She made more calls than *me*.

Exterminated: She made more calls than *I*.

Grammar Gremlin: He speaks as well as *me*.

Exterminated: He speaks as well as *I*.

Grammar Gremlin #4

Misuse of the Pronouns *That* and *Which*

Look for this Grammar Gremlin in your writing. Many people do not know when to use *that* and when to use *which*.

Grammar Gremlin: The report *which* Carol wrote should provide valuable statistics.

Exterminated: The report *that* Carol wrote should provide valuable statistics.

Use *that* to introduce essential or defining clauses. Use *which* to introduce non-essential or non-defining clauses.

Grammar Gremlin: The report on puppy nutrition, *that* Carol finished this morning, should provide valuable statistics.

Exterminated: The report on puppy nutrition, *which* Carol finished this morning, should provide valuable statistics.

Some writers now use *which* (1) when there are two or more parallel essential clauses in the same sentence or (2) when *that* has already been used previously in the sentence.

Grammar Gremlin #5

Misuse of the Pronouns *That* and *Who*

That or *Who?* *Who* or *That?* Good grief! What's a writer to do? This Grammar Gremlin infests many memos, letters, and reports. Let's eradicate it.

Grammar Gremlin: Sam Springer is the only one in our department *that* truly understands dog psychology.

Exterminated: Sam Springer is the only one in our department *who* truly understands dog psychology.

Who and *that* can both refer to persons. However, use *who* when referring to an individual or to the individuality of a group. Use *that* when a class, species, or type is meant.

Grammar Gremlin: Sam is the kind of employee *who* managers want to hire.

Exterminated: Sam is the kind of employee *that* managers want to hire.

Use *that* when referring to places objects and animals.

Grammar Gremlin: Fred is the dog *who* posed for the photo.

Exterminated: Fred is the dog *that* posed for the photo.

Grammar Gremlin #6

Misuse of the Pronouns *Who* and *Whom*

Who or *Whom?* This one causes many writers grief. Don't make it more difficult than it is. All you have to do is remember a couple of simple guidelines.

Grammar Gremlin: *Who* did you meet with today?

Exterminated: *Whom* did you meet with today?

Use *who* whenever *he, she, they, I,* or *we* could replace the *who.* They are all nominative case.

Use *whom* whenever *him, her, them, me,* or *us* can replace the *whom.* They are all objective case.

Still confused? An easy way to ensure that you are using the right form is to rearrange the sentence like this:

> *Whom* did you meet with today? (objective case)
>
> I met with *him* today. (objective case)

Grammar Gremlin: Stan is the one *whom* should attend the conference.

Exterminated: Stan is the one *who* should attend the conference. *(He should attend the conference.)*

Grammar Gremlin: Stan is the one *who* they plan to send.

Exterminated: Stan is the one *whom* they plan to send. (They plan to send *him.)*

Grammar Gremlin #7

Misuse of the Pronoun *Myself*

Me or *Myself?* The guidelines on this one are clear. Nevertheless, I spot these pronoun errors regularly in business documents. I hope you're not guilty of creating this Grammar Gremlin.

Grammar Gremlin: If you have any questions, please call David, Stan, or *myself.*

Exterminated: If you have any questions, please call David, Stan, or *me.*

Never use *myself* in place of *I* or *me. Myself* is a reflexive pronoun and should be used as one.

I attended the conference *myself.*
I thought of the idea *myself.*

Grammar Gremlin: *Myself* and Gray Hound will reveal the new advertising slogan.

Exterminated: Gray Hound and *I* will reveal the new advertising slogan.

Grammar Gremlin #8

Misuse of Indefinite Pronouns: Making Subjects and Verbs Agree in Number

Singular subjects must take singular verbs, and plural subjects must take plural verbs. If they don't, a serious Grammar Gremlin needs exterminating. Make sure you use indefinite pronouns correctly.

Grammar Gremlin: Neither of the employees *are* available.

Exterminated: Neither of the employees *is* available. (Think in terms of *neither one*.)

The pronouns *each, every, either, neither, one,* and *another* are always singular and require a singular verb.

Each of us *is* applying for the promotion.

The pronouns *both, few, many, others*, and *several* are always plural.

> *Both* of us *are* applying for the promotion.

The pronouns *all, none, any, some, more,* and *most* can be singular or plural. It depends on the noun they refer to.

> *None* of the staff *is* applying for the promotion.
> *None* of the employees *are* applying for the promotion.

Grammar Gremlin #9

Misuse of Subject Verb Agreement

A verb form must always agree in number with its subject. That's why it's important to be able to identify both subjects and verbs. Many business writers have these Grammar Gremlins infesting their messages.

Grammar Gremlin: A *variety* of new Bowser Beefy products *are* now on the market.

Exterminated: A *variety* of new Bowser Beefy products *is* now on the market.

The simple subject is *variety.* It is singular and requires a singular verb. Don't let modifying plural words that come between the subject and the verb confuse you. If you do, you will create Grammar Gremlins.

Grammar Gremlin: Five hundred boxes of Doggy Delights *are* a large order for Paws-On Pet Supply.

Exterminated: Five hundred boxes of Doggy Delights *is* a large order for Paws-On Pet Supply.

Most troublesome for many writers is agreement of quantities of distance, time, and amount. Treat them as singular unless you want them interpreted as individual units.

> *Five hundred boxes of Doggy Delights* is considered one order.

Grammar Gremlin #10

Misuse of Subject/Verb Agreement With Compound Subjects

Compound subjects connected by *and* take a plural verb.

> Connie Chow and Carol Collie *work* in Research and Development. (*Work* is the plural form: They *work*/she *works*.)

Singular subjects connected by *or* or *nor* take a singular verb.

> Connie or Carol *writes* the reports.

Grammar Gremlin: Neither the president nor the employees *wants* a labor dispute.

Exterminated: Neither the president nor the employees *want* a labor dispute.

When two subjects differing in number are connected by *either...or,* or *neither...nor* and one of them is plural, it should be placed second and the verb should agree with it in number.

Grammar Gremlin #11

Misuse of the Articles *A* and *An*

Grammar Gremlin: David spoke to the sales representatives for *a* hour.

Exterminated: David spoke to the sales representatives for *an* hour.

Grammar Gremlin: Bill Basenji listened for *an* half-hour and then left.

Exterminated: Bill Basenji listened for *a* half-hour and then left.

If this Grammar Gremlin plagues your memos and letters, follow this general guideline: Consider the sound, not the spelling, of the word following *a* or *an*.

•Use *a* before all consonant sounds, including sounded *h*, long *u*, and *o* with the sound of *w*.

a dog   *a* hound   *a* uniform   *a* CEO

•Use *an* before all vowel sounds except long *u* and before words beginning with a silent *h*.

an empty stomach   *an* honor   *an* RSVP

Grammar Gremlin: Our research team arrived at *a* understanding of the problem.

Exterminated: Our research team arrived at *an* understanding of the problem.

Grammar Gremlin #12

Misuse of Bad and Badly

Grammar Gremlin: Hannah Hound felt *badly* when she lost the Paws for U account.

Exterminated: Hannah Hound felt *bad* when she lost the Paws for U account.

Use the adjective *bad* after the verb *feel* when it functions as a linking verb (a verb that ties what follows to the subject). Verbs of the senses, describing conditions instead of actions, are followed by adjectives. The adverb *badly* follows verbs that show action.

Morton played *badly* in the company softball game.

Morton feels *badly* because he is wearing heavy gloves.

Morton slept *badly* because of the wind.

Think of it like this. If my dog, Fred, smells *bad,* I need to give him a bath. If my dog, Fred, smells *badly,* he has a defective nose.

Grammar Gremlin: Our sales projections for Bowser Beefy's Pup-Time Toys look *badly.*

Exterminated: Our sales projections for Bowser Beefy's Pup-Time Toys look *bad.*

Grammar Gremlin #13

Misuse of *Good* and *Well*

This Grammar Gremlin ravages many business documents, but it is an easy one to exterminate. Follow these guidelines:

- Use *good* as an adjective modifying nouns and pronouns.

   Stan Bernard did a *good* job.

- Use *well* as an adverb. Remember adverbs modify verbs, adjectives, and other adverbs.

   Stan Bernard did *well* on the project.

Grammar Gremlin: The new Pup Pop Tarts taste *well*.

Exterminated: The new Pup Pop Tarts taste *good*.

Just when you think you have it mastered, another problem arises. Use *good* with descriptive verbs (linking) like *look, feel, sound,* and *taste.*

Use *well* with all other verbs.

Grammar Gremlin: Hannah Hound played *good* in the game.

Exterminated: Hannah Hound played *well* in the game.

Also, use *well* when referring to a "state of health." Use *good* when referring to a "state of appearance."

Morton looks *well* this morning. (He's healthy.)

Morton looks *good* this morning. (He's handsome.)

Grammar Gremlin #14

Incorrect Sentence Structure:
Fragments

Use only complete sentences in your business writing and you will avoid this Grammar Gremlin—writing incomplete or fragmented ideas as if they were complete sentences.

Two word groups often appear as sentence fragments. The most common is the clause.

Grammar Gremlin: Because Bill Basenji adjourned the meeting.

Exterminated: Bill Basenji adjourned the meeting.

Exterminated: Because Bill Basenji adjourned the meeting, we stood and left the room.

The other word group—phrases—can also be sentence fragments; however, they aren't as common.

Grammar Gremlin: Sitting at the table.
Exterminated: Bill Basenji is sitting at the table.

Here's a proofreading tip. When checking for fragments, read your sentences out of context. In other words, read your message backwards by reading your last sentence first and working up to your first sentence. Try it! Correct this yourself:

Because our president, David Doberman, stood to speak. We all gave our full attention to him. He announced a new vacation policy effective January 1.

Grammar Gremlin #15

Incorrect Sentence Structure: Run-ons

Don't be guilty of constructing this Grammar Gremlin. You will surely confuse your readers. A run-on sentence is two or more complete sentences run together with no punctuation or with incorrect punctuation. Joining them with only a comma creates a comma splice.

Grammar Gremlin: Rex Shepherd revealed the new slogan, he presented it with much enthusiasm.

Exterminated: Rex Shepherd revealed the new slogan. He presented it to us with much enthusiasm. (Write it as two sentences.)

Exterminated: Rex Shepherd revealed the new slogan, and he presented it with much enthusiasm. (Use a coordinating conjunction with a comma.)

Exterminated: Rex Shepherd revealed the new slogan; he presented it with much enthusiasm. (Use a semicolon.)

Exterminated: Rex Shepherd revealed the new slogan; moreover, he presented it with much enthusiasm. (Use a transition word; place a semicolon before it and a comma after it. See page 39 for a list of transitions.)

Grammar Gremlin #16

Incorrect Sentence Structure: Dangling Participles

Beware! Never, never let your participles dangle. What a strange message you will send to your reader.

Nailed to the door, Betty read the notice.

A participial phrase is a verb form that acts as an adjective modifying a noun or pronoun. If the noun or pronoun is missing or if it is placed so that its relation to the phrase is unclear, the participle "dangles."

Grammar Gremlin: *Filed away for months,* Randy Rottweiler found the sales projections.

Exterminated: Randy Rottweiler found the sales projections that had been filed away for months.

To correct a dangling construction, make the subject of the sentence perform the action expressed in the introductory phrase or clause. That may not always work. You may have to write a completely different sentence.

Grammar Gremlin: *Reading the proposal,* a few problems occurred to me.

Exterminated: As I was reading the proposal, a few problems occurred to me.

Grammar Gremlin #17

Incorrect Sentence Structure: Misplaced Modifiers

Like dangling participles, misplaced modifiers (either words or phrases) provide the basis for unintended (and sometimes humorous) interpretations.

Grammar Gremlin: Wilma Wolf, our CEO, wrote the speech while traveling from Memphis to New York *on the back of a napkin.*

Exterminated: Wilma Wolf, our CEO, wrote her speech *on the back of a napkin* while traveling from Memphis to New York.

Be careful of these Grammar Gremlins. Any message open for interpretation is unacceptable.

Grammar Gremlin: The woman opened the door *with the briefcase.*

Exterminated: The woman *with the briefcase* opened the door.

Grammar Gremlin #18

Incorrect Sentence Structure: Parallel Structure

Parallelism means using similar grammatical structures for similar ideas—matching noun with noun, verb with verb, phrase with phrase, etc. The key to mastering parallel structure is to look for a common denominator. In other words, strive for consistency.

Grammar Gremlin: Wilma Wolf's new secretary is competent and a fast worker. *(Competent* is an adjective, and *a fast worker* is a noun phrase.)

Exterminated: Wilma Wolf's new secretary is competent and fast.

Exterminated: Wilma Wolf's new secretary is a competent, fast worker. (*Competent* and *fast* are both adjectives.)

Grammar Gremlin: Wilma told her to call the conference center and that she should reserve a meeting room. (*To call the conference center* is a phrase, and *that she should reserve a meeting room* is a clause.)

Exterminated: Wilma told her to call the conference center and to reserve a meeting room.

Grammar Gremlin #19

Incorrect Sentence Structure:
Parallel Structure in Lists

By controlling parallel structure, writers add polish and coherence to their documents. On a larger scale, parallelism links ideas together for easy reading.

Grammar Gremlin: We have three tasks to complete before the meeting:

1. By Friday, reserve meeting room.
2. We need to decide on agenda items.
3. Write the agenda and send it to department members.

Exterminated: We have three tasks to complete before the meeting:

1. Reserve a meeting room.
2. Decide on the agenda items.
3. Write the agenda and send it to department members.

Make sure all items in lists are written in the same grammatical structure. The "exterminated" list on this page is written with all verb phrases (fragments). The words at the beginning of the phrases are all present tense, action verbs.

Grammar Gremlin #20

Incorrect Sentence Structure: Placement of *Not Only-But Also* and *Either-Or*

Avoid placing word pairs like *not only...but also* and *either...or* in the wrong sequence.

Grammar Gremlin: Iris Setter is *not only* proficient in word processing *but also* in desktop publishing.

Exterminated: Iris Setter is proficient *not only* in word processing *but also* in desktop publishing.

Grammar Gremlin: Randy Rottweiler is *either* planning to apply for General Manager *or* Vice-President.

Exterminated: Randy Rottweiler is plan-
ning to apply for *either*
General Manager *or* Vice-
President.

Make sure to place all words and phrases correctly in the sentence. Your message will read
clearly, smoothly, and accurately.

Grammar Gremlin #21

Incorrect Use of Prepositions

Did you ever learn the rule "Never end a sentence with a preposition"? If so, you can unlearn it. Learn this rule: Don't use prepositions unnecessarily.

Grammar Gremlin: Where is the research department *at?*

Exterminated: Where is the research department?

Whether or not a sentence should end with a preposition depends on the emphasis or level or formality you want.

> FORMAL: David did not understand *about* what she was talking.
>
> INFORMAL (better): David did not understand what she was talking *about*.

FORMAL: *In* which chapter will she find the information?

INFORMAL (better) Which chapter will she find the information *in?*

As you can see, sometimes prepositions are good words to end sentences with.

Grammar Gremlin #22

Use of Double Negatives

Remember this simple rule: Don't use no double negatives. OOPS! That's a Grammar Gremlin contaminating this message. Let's try it again. Remember this simple rule: Don't use any double negatives.

Grammar Gremlin: David and Wilma *don't* have *nothing* to worry about.

Exterminated: David and Wilma *don't* have *anything* to worry about.

Exterminated: David and Wilma *have nothing* to worry about.

Negatives are *no, not, nor neither, none, never, no one, hardly*, and *scarcely*. Don't use more than one of them in the same clause.

Grammar Gremlin: The new Bowser Beefy slogan must be kept secret; therefore, *don't* reveal it to *nobody*.

Exterminated: The new Bowser Beefy slogan must be kept secret; therefore, *don't* reveal it to *anybody*.

Grammar Gremlin #23

Incorrect Expression of Numbers in Dates

Grammar Gremlin: Bowser Beefy Dog Food Company, Inc., announced the new slogan on April *1st*, 1994. They introduced their new product line on July *12th*, 1994.

Exterminated: Bowser Beefy Dog Food Company, Inc., announced the new slogan on April *1*, 1994. They introduced their new product line on July *12*, 1994.

When the day follows the month, use a numerical *(1, 2, 3, 4, 5, 6, 7, 8, 9, 10, etc.)*. Do not add -*st*, -*nd*, -*rd*, -*th* to the number.

However, when the day precedes the month, or stands alone, you can write it in either the numerical (*lst, 2nd, 3rd,* etc.) or as a word (*first, second, third,* etc.)

> Bowser Beefy Dog Food Company, Inc., announced the new slogan on the *1st* of April.

A NOTE: It's preferable to write *April 1,* not the *lst of April.*

Grammar Gremlin #24

Incorrect Comparatives and Superlatives

Grammar Gremlin: David Doberman's explanation of the new benefits program was *more clear* than Stan Bernard's.

Exterminated: David Doberman's explanation of the new benefits program was *clearer* than Stan Bernard's.

As a general rule, form the comparative degree of one-syllable adjectives and adverbs by adding *-er* to them. Form the superlative by adding *-est*.

However, you will find some exceptions.

Grammar Gremlin: The brainstorming activity was *funner* than the introductory activity.

Exterminated: The brainstorming activity was *more fun* than the introductory activity.

Form the comparative degree of two-syllable adjectives and adverbs by adding *-er* or by using the word *more*. Form the superlative by using *-est* or the word *most*. Most of the time you will use *-er* or *-est*.

happy   *(happier, more happy)*
tasty   *(tastier, more tasty)*
likely   *(likeliest, most likely)*

Form the comparative and superlative degrees of words that have three or more syllables by using the words *more* or *most*.

reliable   *(more reliable)*
interesting   *(most interesting)*

Other Problems

Grammar Gremlin: Ima Mutt is the *most* competent of the two candidates we interviewed.

Exterminated: Ima Mutt is the *more* competent of the two candidates we interviewed.

Use the comparative form *more* when referring to two persons, places, or things. Use the superlative form *most* when referring to three or more persons, places, or things.

Grammar Gremlin: Ima Mutt's description was *more clearer* than mine.

Exterminated: Ima Mutt's description was *clearer* than mine.

Be sure not to use double comparisons. This Grammar Gremlin will surely make you sound uneducated.

Grammar Gremlin #25

Use of Nonstandard Words Like
Irregardless

If you want to appear illiterate, use words that don't exist. *Irregardless* is one of those words.

Grammar Gremlin: *Irregardless* of the situation, we will announce the new slogan tomorrow morning. It is "Beef Up Bowser With Bowser Beefy."

Exterminated: *Regardless* of the situation, we will announce the new slogan tomorrow morning. It is "Beef Up Bowser With Bowser Beefy."

Kick those Grammar Gremlins out of your language and out of your life. Chase them off of every page of your writing. You'll be more confident about the words you use and the effectiveness of their placement in a sentence.

Remember, what you put on paper makes a powerful impression. Make sure yours is a superior one.

Don't juggle the troublesome *who* or *whom*.

About the Author

With Jean Rupp's help, you don't have to work like a dog to write like a pro. Jean is the founder and president of Write Communications, a consulting and training company in Portland, Oregon. She provides corporations, government, and colleges with workshops and seminars in effective business writing and communication skills. In her long list of satisfied clients are Fortune 500 companies like Nike, Inc., PacifiCorp, and Tektronix, Inc.

Because of Jean's special talent helping business people communicate clearly and concisely, she has been included in *Marquis Who's Who in the West* (23rd and 24th Editions) and *Marquis Who's Who in Finance and Industry.* You also will find her listed in *Who's Who in Professional Speaking.*

Index

To contact Jean Rupp for workshops,
seminars or consultations:
503-292-2511

~ ~ ~

To order additional copies of
Grammar Gremlins

Please send ____ copies at $9.95 each book,
plus $2.50 shipping and handling for the first
book, $1.50 for each additional book in the
same order.

Enclosed is my check of money order for
$_____ or [ ] Visa   [ ] MasterCard
_____Exp. ____/____
Signature _____
Phone _____
Name _____
Address _____
City/St/Zip _____
(Advise if recipient and mailing address
are different from above.)

Return this order form to:
BookPartners, Inc.
P.O. Box 922
Wilsonville, Oregon 97070
503-682-9821